RUNNING THE COURSE

*Becoming a Champion
in God's Eyes*

KRISTI OVERTON JOHNSON

DEDICATION

This book is dedicated to my loving husband and best friend, Tim, and to my dear little one, Ty. Thank you both for your love and the joy that you bring into my life. I love you more than you'll ever know!

RUNNING THE COURSE
Copyright © 2003 by Kristi Overton Johnson
All rights reserved
Printed in the United States of America
0-8054-3048-2

Published by Broadman & Holman Publishers
Nashville, Tennessee
www.broadmanholman.com

Dewey Decimal Classification: 248.4
Subject Heading: SPIRITUAL LIFE \ WATER SPORTS

Photography Credits:
Tom King: front cover, pages 28, 53, 55, 67, 70, 75, 76, 89, 91, 117, 123, 129, 132, 133, 137, 138, 148, 151.
Overton's: pages 3, 8, 9, 10, 13, 14, 18, 21, 22, 24, 59, 88, 95, 109.
Joey Meddock: pages 7, 19, 29, 44, 47, 54, 82, 90, 93, 104, 110, 126, 127, 144, 145, 153.
Bill Doster: pages 11, 27, 34, 37, 49, 58, 64, 68, 69,72, 99, 101, 102, 111, 113, 125, 134, 135, 139.
Bruce Neville: page 17.
Scott Atkinson: pages 26, 40, 65, 71, 73, 79, 103, 114, 122.
Dean Collins: pages 30, 31, 106, 147.
Correct Craft: pages 33, 39, 57, 77, 83, 85, 94, 98, 118, 119, 121, 131, 136, 143, 152.
John Linn: pages 43, 80.
World Publications: pages 63, 149.
Josh Letchworth: page 87.
Ross Outerbridge: pages 141, 142, 154.

My first exposure to waterskiing was at camp in the 1960s. Like millions of others, the lasting memory is of water in my mouth, nose, and lungs, as the instructor kept yelling at me to keep my legs bent and arms straight. I remember the roar of the engine, the jerk of the rope, and multiple near-death experiences. I gave up. To this day, I've never learned to water-ski.

So what is it that Kristi Overton Johnson, professional skier, and Franklin Graham have in common? Not much when it comes to skiing. But we do share a common faith in the Lord Jesus Christ. Kristi has faithfully exhibited Christ's love through what she does, and her life is making a difference. Isn't that what all of us should be doing with the lives God gives us? I believe you'll be inspired and challenged through the pages of *Running the Course*.

–Franklin Graham
Samaritan's Purse

Kristi is someone who has achieved a great deal in athletics and life. As in my case, she's learned a lot about life's lessons through athletics, and Kristi has accepted God as the right Coach for her life, which goes right along with my life's philosophy. Life is the biggest game of all, and none of us wants to lose the biggest game we'll ever play in.

It is always fun for me to study the lives of people who are successful in other athletic venues and watch how they use their success to reach others. My experience has been that those who follow God's game plan—which is laid out in the Bible—end up not only with vocational success but also achieve personal success and a well-rounded life. Without question, I believe Kristi, with God as her Coach, is succeeding in all areas of her life. As you "run the course" with Kristi, consider asking God to be your Coach for life.

–Joe Gibbs
Owner of Joe Gibbs Racing

Contents

Chapter 1: Get Off the Dock! 7

Chapter 2: Out of the Water 21

Chapter 3: Who's Your Coach? 39

Chapter 4: Preparing for God's Course 53

Chapter 5: One Buoy at a Time 67

Chapter 6: Your Spiritual Keys 79

Chapter 7: Let Go of the Controls 93

Chapter 8: Take It to the Next Level 109

Chapter 9: Get Up When You Fall 125

Chapter 10: Finishing Well 141

GET OFF THE DOCK!

Picture the morning sun shining its light on an absolutely still lake, fog rising from the water, neon slalom buoys perfectly aligned, and a boat waiting faithfully at the dock. Can there be anything more beautiful?

Not if you are looking through the eyes of a water-skier.

Every morning as I draw open my curtains, I am blessed to witness this description of beauty. It is a sight that stirs many emotions within me . . .

Peace and hope—knowing I have been given another day, another chance to live life to its fullest.

Thankfulness—for the awesome life God has afforded me as a professional athlete.

Excitement—as I look out at the buoys and wonder if today will be the day that I go deeper into that course than ever before.

Even after decades of waterskiing, I still have difficulty resisting my urge to carve through the morning's virgin water. If you're an early morning fisherman—sorry! But the water calls my name, and I just can't resist experiencing it again and again and again.

Sound crazy? Perhaps to some, but for thousands of enthusiasts like me, waterskiing is a big part of our lives. The perfect alignment of neon-colored buoys is like a work of art. The roar of the boat's engine is like music to our ears.

You may be wondering how one's interpretation of beauty can become so warped. For me, it all began with one simple event: getting up on a pair of water skis for the first time.

Love at First Sight

Although I was only four years old, I can still vividly remember the excitement of being pulled up and down the shoreline on little training skis, to the clapping and cheering of my family and friends. I even remember thinking, right then and there, that I always wanted to learn something new every time I took to the water.

Little did I know how this desire would affect my life. Never in my wildest dreams could I imagine that I would become a world record holder for more than a decade. Nor could I imagine that twenty-nine years after my first skiing experience, I would still be competing and making a living doing something I love to do.

Reaching the top of the sport of waterskiing didn't come easy. Granddaddy Charlie always said it would take a long time to be a waterskiing champion . . . and it did. It required sacrifices that were often difficult to make, especially as a child. There was no such thing as a lazy summer for me! Every day was *practice, practice, practice*—not just in the summer, but on most days after school. Practically everything in my life from the time I was a child—even today, as an adult—has revolved around waterskiing: the things I eat, the places I go, the people I'm around.

Yet I wasn't the only one making sacrifices. Although waterskiing is an individual sport, it still takes a team of people to make it all possible. For me, that team consisted of my parents, Parker and Becky Overton, and my brother, Michael.

As I look back, I'm amazed and humbled by both the personal and the financial sacrifices my family made so that my dream of becoming a world champion water-skier could come to fruition. My father worked hard to provide me with the best opportunities. He even went so far as to build me my own lake, Lake Kristi, so that I could train without the stings of jellyfish, the disturbance of other boaters, and the choppy waters of a large river. I know it may sound a bit strange, but when you're twelve years old, you don't realize that having your own lake is unusual. *Didn't everyone grow up with a lake in her back yard?*

Staying Up

Yet even with a devoted family and all the opportunities afforded to me, taking to the water each day was still something I had to do myself.

I'll admit, in the early years my father often bribed me. Toys and dollar bills were sometimes offered in exchange for mastering a new trick or performing my best in competition. But even then, I still had to get out on the water and learn! No one could ski for me. No one could make me want to be the best.

I had to have the desire and the discipline to get up after each fall and try to do better.

I had to be humble enough to accept the coaching of others and try what they were telling me to do on the water.

I had to keep pushing myself even when I wanted to climb in the boat for the last time.

There have been times when I wanted to hang up my skis and end my professional skiing career. Sure, there have been many victories, but also just as many disappointments: unfair conditions at tournaments, unbelievable judgment calls, unfortunate injuries, equipment failure . . . the list could go on and on. With every win, it seems, defeat soon follows. One day I can navigate my way through the slalom course with ease; the very next set, it feels like I've never been on a ski before in my life!

But regardless of the sacrifices and the frustrations of waterskiing, something inside of me keeps pushing me to put that ski back on and give it another whirl.

But Why?

While writing these pages, I've spent many hours trying to pinpoint the true motivation behind my life's devotion to waterskiing: why I've spent hours upon hours on the water—often in the company of alligators and snakes; why I've traveled all over the world and spent tens of thousands of dollars a year just for a

- *I had to have the desire and the discipline*

- *I had to be humble enough*

- *I had to keep pushing myself*

What makes us do it?

- Is it the exercise?
- Is it the mental challenge?
- Is it the hunger to improve?

couple of minutes on the water; why I've continued to ski when it often poses a health risk and is against the advice of doctors.

Well, for many of you reading this book, you know why. After you've experienced the wind on your cheeks, the speed of the boat, and the sound of the ski slicing through the water, you just can't help but be drawn back to the water time and time again. Add to these the excitement of mastering a new skill and the burning of your muscles after a great set, and you're hooked! Many of you are probably even guilty of *breaking through the ice* so you can get a jump on the competition (now, even *I* am not *that* committed to skiing!).

But what makes us do it? What makes us choose to spend our entire lives chasing after little orange buoys on a water ski?

Is it the exercise? It does provide a great, overall body workout in just minutes! For those of us who hate spending hours in the gym, waterskiing provides a quick, fun, and effective way to build muscle.

Is it the mental challenge? Being able to master new skills while a boat is playing tug-of-war with your body takes great concentration. Not only that, but you're always at the mercy of the weather, other boaters, and your driver. It's a true experience!

Is it the hunger to improve? I know that even as the world record holder, I haven't reached my potential. There's always one more buoy to round, one rope-length shorter to go, one more title to obtain. I am never satisfied! Therefore, I keep pushing myself to new limits so that I can accomplish feats I once only dreamed were possible.

What If?

It's not easy to explain this motivation we feel. But one thing I do know: My life would be totally different today if I hadn't gotten off the dock at age four and entered the world of waterskiing.

What if I had given up after my first fall? What if I had told my parents, "You know, I think I've skied enough for today. I just want to go back to the shore and play with my friends."

I definitely would have missed out on a lot of adventures. I never would have experienced the thrill of crossing the wakes at seventy miles an hour, soaring through the air on jump skis, or performing the awesome tricks people love to see. I might never have had the opportunity to travel so extensively and meet people from all over the globe. I almost certainly would never have experienced the sheer sense of patriotism I felt while watching the American flag rise above my head as the National Anthem echoed across foreign waters.

No, my life wouldn't have been the same.

Yet I still wonder: Why have I put so much effort into a sport that is supposed to be just for fun? Time, money, and physical sacrifices—all for a feeling of joy and exhilaration.

Kristi with Granddaddy Charlie

As a Christian, I can't help but think how misplaced my efforts have often been. In many ways I've spent my life chasing a sense of satisfaction that has proven to be only temporary. If I had put forth the same effort as a teenager in chasing after the *permanent* joy that a relationship with Jesus Christ can provide, I'm certain that as a young adult, my life would have been dramatically different. I'm also certain that God would have used me to greatly affect many more people along the way. I can only imagine where I would be today–spiritually–if I had invested the same commitment into knowing Christ as I have in rounding buoys, jumping ramps, and learning tricks.

Unfortunately, though, as a young Christian I didn't have the same dedication, passion, and determination in my relationship with the Lord as I did on the water. Yes, I was blessed to be raised in a Christian home. My parents took me to church every time the doors were open. They even enrolled me in a Christian school. Just as in skiing, I was afforded many opportunities. I was given all I needed in order to have an incredible relationship with God. But I never made that personal commitment to chase after a relationship with Him like I chased after waterskiing titles.

Sitting on the Dock

When I was an eight-year-old girl, I received Jesus into my heart and was baptized. I knew the basics of Christianity: God coming to this earth in the form of a man named Jesus Christ, His going to the cross to pay the penalty for my sins, His resurrection from the dead. I believed every word of it.

But I didn't really understand how these things should impact my life. I didn't realize that Jesus wanted more from me than belief, that He wanted me to know Him personally, the way I know my friends and family . . . intimately! I also didn't understand that my belief in Christ should result in a total, daily surrender of my life to Him, a complete abandonment of my own personal desires—full obedience. I didn't see that my faith in God should affect every area of my life, every decision I make, every word I speak, and everything I do (just like my pursuit of becoming a champion water-skier). Therefore, I failed to make the commitment to grow and mature in Christ.

Basically, I sat right down on a "spiritual dock" and didn't move. I was like a skier who believes in her ability, buys all the right gear, and gets ready to go, but never actually jumps in the water to experience all it has to offer. She foregoes the excitement of being pulled out of the water by the powerful boat, the speed of the skis, and the thrill of performing tricks. Because of pride, fear of the unknown, or the sense of contentment she feels while lying on the dock, she never grabs hold of the rope and goes with the boat when it comes around to pick her up. She assumes she will be able to ski some other time, never stopping to think that the opportunity to ski may never come again. The weather may turn bad, the crew may get tired, or the boat may even run out of gas!

If I had put forth the same effort as a teenager in chasing after the *permanent* joy that a relationship with Jesus Christ can provide, I'm certain that as a young adult, my life would have been dramatically different.

For twelve years I was like that skier—watching from the dock, putting my spiritual life on hold by refusing to enter the water with God. I let my pride and my fear of relinquishing control keep me from experiencing the excitement of living with Christ.

Oh, I would occasionally jump off the dock, so to speak. I'd ski around spiritually a little bit, looking and feeling like I was a Christian. But I didn't see the urgency of chasing after a relationship with Christ. I knew I believed in Him. I had been baptized. I went to church. I even talked to large groups of people about Jesus.

Could there be more to being a Christian?

Living Water

Oh, if only I had known then what I know now! My dear friend, there is so much more to life than what I was experiencing—so much more to being a Christian than I realized.

When I finally got off that spiritual dock in my early twenties, my life was forever changed. When I started putting forth just a smidgen of the same effort in my Christian walk as I did on the water, I saw incredible results.

I began to experience God's power in my life as I watched Him at work all around me.

I started to feel His presence daily as I witnessed events only He could orchestrate.

I began to hear His voice guiding me in every decision I had to make.

When I finally got off that spiritual dock in my early twenties, my life was forever changed.

And I experienced a transformation of my mind that allowed me to experience the "abundant" or "full" life God refers to in John 10:10, a life consisting of inner joy, hope, peace, and love.

It was all there. I had just been searching for it in the wrong place! All it took was a desire, a commitment on my part to develop a relationship with God, to get into His Word daily, to choose to be obedient to Him. He was there all along, waiting for me to grab hold of the rope so that He could pull me out of life's choppy waters and into the course He had orchestrated for my life.

How about you?

Have you been searching for a level of joy, hope, peace, love, and security you could count on to stay constant no matter what your circumstances? Have you been wondering if there is more to life than what you are experiencing?

If you have, there is no need to search any longer. God is right here, beside you, right now. He is waiting for you to grab hold of Him so that you can experience His abundant life.

Just as I had to make a personal decision to dedicate myself to becoming a champion water-skier, you will have to make the decision yourself to be a champion for Christ. No one can make you want it, and no one can do it for you. God is ready and willing to change your life, to use you in exciting and unimaginable ways.

Don't do as I once did. Don't be like the skier who's content to stay on the dock and watch from the sidelines. Never assume that you will always have the opportunity to develop a relationship with God later in life. The truth is, you may never again have the opportunity to come to know Him. But even if you can, why would you want to forfeit the boatload of blessings God has waiting for you today?

So please don't wait. Get off the dock and go with God.

Don't be like the skier who's content to stay on the dock and watch from the sidelines.

How?

Hopefully by now you're saying, "Yes, I want a more fulfilling life. I want a life of hope, joy, and peace regardless of my circumstances. I want God to navigate me through the course He has prepared for me!"

But you may be asking a lot of *how* questions:

"How do I begin?"

"How will I be able to find the time?"

"How will He ever be able to use me?"

"How will I know if I'm on the right track?"

"How will I stay focused on Him with all the distractions in my life?"

In the following chapters of this book, I'm going to try to answer these questions based on my experiences in walking with Christ. No, I'm not an expert in theology, but I've experienced God at work in my life, and He is teaching me new things every day. Even in writing this book, He has revealed new truths to me about Himself, His character, and His love that have helped me in my own pursuit of becoming a champion for Him. It is my prayer that through the use of the wonderful ski analogies He has brought to my mind, you will be able to more clearly understand how you can have a better relationship with Christ.

Who knows, you may even find a ski tip or two in these pages!

But before we go any further, take this moment to examine your life. Go ahead. Pray right now that God will give you the courage and strength to let go of whatever you're holding on to—whether it's your pride, your dreams, whatever—and grab hold of Him so you can experience a complete life in Christ, running the course He has prepared for you.

My prayer for you as you read the pages of this book is fourfold:

• I pray you will desire to know Him better every day of your life.

• I pray you will always seek to know Him more.

• I pray that no matter what the cost, you will dedicate your life to becoming more like Him.

Please don't wait. Get off the dock and go with God.

• And lastly, I pray you will go into your mission fields (your home and workplace) with excitement, sharing with others how God is working in your life. Let's not reserve our excitement for personal bests on the water!

Are you ready to get started becoming a champion for Christ?

God has some great and mighty plans for you, "plans for well-being, not for disaster, to give you a future and hope" (Jeremiah 29:11). So let's not waste any more time. Come with me as we get off our spiritual docks and begin experiencing what it means to ski on God's course. Let us take to the water of Christian living with excitement and commitment, so that when we reach the end of our journey, we will receive the most wonderful praise of all: "Well done, . . . You were faithful over a few things; I will put you in charge of many things. Enter your master's joy!" (Matthew 25:21).

Prayer

Dear Lord, examine my heart, mind, and life. If I am sitting on a spiritual dock, help me to get up, to get over my fears and doubts, and go with You. I don't want to be content where I am any longer. I want to know You more intimately every day of my life. Forgive me for putting my own desires and dreams ahead of my relationship with You. I know that everything done here on earth without You in mind is meaningless, a chasing after the wind. I want the lasting joy, true excitement, and unexplainable peace that can only come from You. I know You have wonderful plans for me, and I want to experience all You have in store. Help me today as I embark on my lifelong journey of becoming a champion for You! Amen.

CHAPTER 2

OUT OF THE WATER

Do you remember the day you really *became* a water-skier? I do.

For me, it happened in the summer of 1974 on the beaches of the Pamlico River, near Washington, North Carolina.

I was just four years old, and eager to get out on the water. All my life I had watched my parents skiing—well, OK, all four years of my life!—but even at such a young age, I could see how much fun they were having, and I wanted to experience it too. So my family and friends tied my skis together to help me control them, then tied a rope to the skis, and began pulling me up and down the shoreline of the beach.

I loved skiing from that very moment—with an immediate enthusiasm for the sport that made me want to get better and better at it every day. Within no time I had outgrown my training skis and had moved on to combos. At the age of five, I shed one ski altogether and became a slalom skier. And from that day to this, I've spent my life trying to master the slalom course.

No, I'll never forget that day!

But just as I can pinpoint the moment I became a water-skier, I can also pinpoint the day when Jesus Christ became the Lord of my life—the day I dedicated my life to serving Him.

It was the summer of 1995. I was doing some ski instruction at the Word of Life Camp in Schroon Lake, New York. And one night—on stage in front of about five hundred teenagers, sharing with them about how they could use their talents to bring glory to God—the Lord caught the words right in my throat . . . and asked me if I was listening to what I was saying.

Who? Me?

I will never forget the tug on my heart as I stood there, looking into the faces of those teenagers, yet at the same time feeling as if Jesus was standing right beside me, telling me that I needed to get right with Him.

Even as I spoke, I began to reflect on what I had witnessed during that week: excited children full of joy and singing praise songs, devoted kids gathering prayerfully in small groups to study the Bible, tears of repentance flowing as the Lord opened their hearts to the many things in their lives that were keeping them from living freely with Him.

I had to ask myself: Did I have that same kind of joy and excitement, that kind of devotion, that kind of repentant attitude? Yet here I stood before hundreds of hearts and minds, sharing what God was doing in my life, trying to tell them how to live their lives for Jesus, when I didn't even know what that meant myself.

I couldn't help but feel a twinge of guilt. I had come to tell these teenagers about the Lord, yet they had introduced me to Him. God had brought me to that youth camp not so much to help others but to make me really want to seek Him and to know Him.

Isn't it amazing how He will use situations like that to get our attention?

So when I got back to my cabin that night, I got on my knees and surrendered my life to Christ. I asked forgiveness for being such a hypocrite, and invited God to take control of my life and to lead me wherever He wanted me to go. I began a new and exciting course God had prepared for me.

And just as I had promised at four years of age to improve my skiing every day, I also made a vow to God that night—a promise to know Him better and to serve Him more . . . every day.

Here I stood before hundreds of hearts and minds, sharing what God was doing in my life, trying to tell them how to live their lives for Jesus, when I didn't even know what that meant myself.

All I wanted as a child was to fit in, to be normal . . . I was claiming to be a Christian, yet at the same time, I could easily do without Him when it served me to do so.

All Dressed Up

I'm not sure why it happened this way. I was blessed to grow up in a Christian home, and I attended church my whole life. I had heard all about Jesus, His death, and His resurrection. I had even walked an aisle to the front of our church one day at the age of eight to publicly profess my belief in Him. Yet outside of the fact that I knew God had given me a talent to water-ski, I didn't really know much else about Him.

Maybe that's because waterskiing was all I had on my mind. For while I was willing to practice my sport like crazy every day, I was content with remaining on my spiritual training skis as a Christian . . . never growing, never maturing, never stretching my limits to see what was out there.

Many of you know just what I'm talking about. Like I did, you may call yourself a Christian, but you know in your heart that you haven't yet made Him Lord over your life. You've never really stepped out on what they call the "Christian walk"—a term that describes movement, going forward in your relationship with God, learning more about Him as you live each day with Him at your side.

Does that make you as sad as it made me when I discovered it—just imagining how many lives could have been pointed to Jesus if only I'd made the commitment early on to live for Him?

Unfortunately, though, I was much more committed to pleasing the world around me than pleasing Christ. All I wanted as a child was to fit in, to be normal.

I never wanted people to think that I thought of myself in some high-and-mighty way just because I was a successful water-skier. But this desire to please everyone was ruining my Christian testimony. I was claiming to be a Christian, yet at the same time, I could easily do without Him when it served me to do so.

But when God humbled me on the stage that night, He showed me that He can see straight through to our hearts. We may be able to fool others—even ourselves!—by claiming to be Christians and by doing all the right things, like going to church or helping those in need. But we can't fool God. He knows our thoughts and the desires of our hearts. He knows whether we've truly committed our lives to Him.

It's What's on the Inside

Skis have this same kind of quality about them. As a professional water-skier, I've tried hundreds of skis in my career. And for the most part, they all look the same from the outside. The graphics are beautiful, the bindings are new, and the fin is bright and shiny. But I'm here to tell you that not all skis are the same! I can receive two skis from the same company, in fact, and they will often be completely different. One may be a really good ski, and the other may get tossed into my garage or made into a mailbox post.

What really matters is how they are "laid up" on the inside.

The way the carbon, glass, and fiberglass are placed into them can make all the difference in the world, giving the ski its strength and its ability to take the pressure that the skier places on it in the turns. The varying amounts of these

elements also determine the ski's speed behind the boat and how it will be able to accelerate and decelerate at the proper times.

Some skis have it and some don't. But their worth has very little to do with the outside package. Just about everything of value in a water ski is what's found on the inside.

Isn't it like that with us, too? Although we basically all look the same on the outside, it's who we are on the inside that determines whether we are "laid up" correctly. If our hearts are not full of Jesus Christ, we will simply snap when the world applies its pressure.

First Samuel 16:7 says, "Man sees what is visible, but the LORD sees the heart." Nothing we do, say, or even think can be hidden from Him. "All things are naked and exposed to the eyes of Him to whom we must give an account" (Hebrews 4:13). And one day, every one of us will stand before God and be seen for who we are on the inside. But only those who have received Christ as their Lord and Savior, whose names are written in the Lamb's Book of Life, "whose lawless acts are forgiven and whose sins are covered" by the blood of Jesus Christ will be able to stand there with hearts that are clean and pure. "Blessed is the man whose sin the Lord will never charge against him." (Romans 4:7–8).

Praise God!

Oh, I am so thankful God tugged at my heart that night on the stage, and that I responded to Him. I would hate to think that I could have gone throughout my whole life assuming I was a Christian, yet when it was all said and done, I would have been denied entrance to heaven. But that's what would have happened to me had I not finally given my life over to Jesus and begun living for Him.

I would have been like the slalom skier who made a world record run but was still disqualified . . . for missing the gate.

The Entrance Gate

If you've not yet tried course skiing or don't know the rules, here's how it works: The course consists of a set of entrance and exit gates, plus six buoys that the skier must round. The winner of the event is the one who runs the most consecutive buoys at the shortest length of rope.

The elements are the same for each skier. The boat speed remains constant, and the buoys are in the same position for everyone. There is basically only one error that can cause a skier to be disqualified: missing the entrance gates.

In competition a gate judge determines whether the skier went through the gates. Any skier who misses them is disqualified regardless of how many buoys he runs. Oftentimes the skier will argue with the judge that he or she made the gates. But the judge's call stands, and the skier isn't allowed to go any farther.

There has often been talk among skiers that the gates should be eliminated from the course altogether or—at the least—the skier should be given a bigger tolerance. Some skiers claim that the gates really shouldn't matter at all as long as the person completes the course.

Don't we often hear that same argument made in terms of religion? People say that there really isn't an entrance gate into heaven, just a course of life we all must complete. Many believe that as long as a person does good things and lives a good life, that should be enough. The Bible, however, is clear that the gates cannot be missed or ignored if one desires to enter the kingdom of heaven. Yes, life is a course with many twists and turns, but no matter how cleanly we run the course, if we miss the gates, our lives will not count for eternity.

Titus 3:5 says "He saved us—not by works of righteousness that we had done, but according to His mercy." We are saved by His grace and not because of anything we have done, lest we boast in ourselves and our achievements (Ephesians 2:8–9).

It is impossible to work our way into heaven. We are saved only through faith in Jesus Christ. He is the one and only entrance gate, and God the Father is our gate judge. He ultimately knows whether we made the gates or not—whether we have accepted His gift of forgiveness and made Him Lord over our lives. The Bible says in Matthew 7:21, "Not everyone who says to Me, 'Lord, Lord!' will enter the kingdom of heaven." Many people will think they made the gates, but just like in skiing, the Judge's call will stand.

I know how I might have responded to this harsh-sounding statement at one point in my life. "But wait, Lord, I went to church. I had Christian parents. I believed You existed. I even went around telling people to live their lives for You." That could have been me. That would have been all I'd have had to fall back on. Yet I would have heard Him respond, "I never knew you" (Matthew 7:23), because He wasn't really my Lord. I was living life on my own . . . for my own personal glory.

A Second Chance

I'll never forget the 1999 World Championships in Milan, Italy. I was skiing well—coming into the fourth buoy—any part of buoy five and I would be the world champion. Then suddenly, something happened and I knew that there was no way that I was going to take the title during this run. My focus shifted from thoughts of a win to making sure that I tied my dear friends Toni Neville and Susi Graham so that I could stay in the hunt for the gold.

It is impossible to work our way into heaven. We are saved only through faith in Jesus Christ. He is the one and only entrance gate, and God the Father is our gate judge.

Fortunately, I had just enough speed to cross the first wake. But when I looked up toward the boat, all I saw was an enormous amount of slack line. Oh no, I thought, here it comes! I buckled down, held on tight, then began to say a quick prayer for my neck and back just as I was yanked right out of my ski.

In a flash, unexpectedly, I was down. Had I totally blown it?

In slalom skiing (as you may know) the amount of buoys the skier runs is determined by the judges. The winner, of course, is the skier who rounds the most at the shortest length of rope. This may seem cut-and-dried, but the judges actually can award whole, half, or quarter buoys. Many times I've won (or lost) by as little as a quarter buoy. But the rule reads that as long as the skier crosses the first wake with the rope in her hand, she's awarded a full buoy.

And a full four buoys was what I had to have in order to tie Toni and Susi and force a runoff.

But the judges were so far away from the course, I wasn't sure for a minute (or what seemed like an hour!) if they'd seen my ski cross the wake. All I could do was just sit in the water . . . and wait.

Finally, the announcer's voice came over the intercom and boomed out in Italian: *Quatra buoys!* I knew enough Italian to know that *quatra* meant four. I had tied my friends! I could try again to win the gold!

I will never forget how relieved I felt. I had been given a second chance to win the tournament. But I also remember having some emotions of guilt. What if my friends and competitors didn't think I deserved the full buoy? What if they didn't think I had crossed the wake?

As I wrestled with these emotions, I remember hearing my father's distinct Southern accent coming from the crowded Italian shoreline. He had pushed his way through thousands of spectators to the water's edge and was yelling at the top of his lungs, "You can do it, baby!"

My father was there, encouraging me to get up and try again. He believed in me, he believed in the judge's call, and he believed in my ability to win the event.

Try It Again

What a beautiful sight! My father was cheering me on, encouraging me, and wanting wonderful things for me. He and my mother have always been there for me, believing in me and pushing me to be the best. They believed in me when I didn't even believe in myself.

But how much more is our heavenly Father cheering us on, running up and down the banks of our lives saying, "You can do it, my child! I believe in you! I love you, and I want you to have a second chance to experience life in its fullest!" Can't you just hear His distinct voice encouraging you to accept His gift of life?

That's what God desires for every one of us—to come to Him and receive this second chance. In fact, all of heaven rejoices "over one sinner who repents" and receives His gift of salvation (Luke 15:10). We don't deserve His love. We don't deserve His mercy and encouragement. We don't deserve a second chance. We are sinners who fall short of His perfect standard (Romans 3:23). We fall short of crossing the first wake on a daily basis. But like those judges, He gives us a second chance.

How much more is our heavenly Father cheering us on, running up and down the banks of our lives saying, "You can do it, my child! I believe in you! I love you, and I want you to have a second chance to experience life in its fullest!"

I am so thankful that I serve a loving, merciful, and forgiving God—a God of second chances. I am forever grateful for the second chance He has given me at a fulfilling life here on earth and eternal life with Him in heaven. This second chance has been kind of like getting a mulligan in a golf game or a re-ride in a ski competition. Although we have fallen short of winning the prize, we are given another try.

I think of how grateful I felt for getting a second chance in that ski tournament, a second chance for something I had earned. But how much more grateful I should feel for my second chance at *salvation*, something I fall short of deserving *every day!*

That is the grace of God—His giving to us something so undeserved, yet so beautiful. All we have to do to receive His gift is acknowledge that we are not worthy of it, that we cannot do anything on our own to save ourselves, and ask Him to come into our lives and give us a second chance.

The Rope, Please

Can you imagine, though, if when the boat came around to get me at the World Championships, I had told the driver, "Thanks for offering, but I'm not interested. I can do this on my own. I don't need a boat to get me through the course." Or maybe, "To tell you the truth, I don't think I even *want* a second chance to win this tournament. I'd rather just stay out here in the water and swim awhile."

The driver would have thought I had lost my mind! Never in a million years would I have said those things. I wanted more than anything to go with the

That is the grace of God—His giving to us something so undeserved, yet so beautiful.

boat and have a second chance at the win. Yet the only way I could get connected to the power source that had the ability to pull me out of the water and through the course was to set aside my fears, guilt, and pride and *grab hold of that rope!*

Well, Jesus is like that rope. And the only way we can get connected to God, who is sort of like our ski boat, is by being willing to put our trust in the rope, Jesus Christ. Jesus is the only way to be connected to the ultimate source of power.

Like the boat, God is there beside us, and He is willing to guide us and lead us through life. We're not forced to follow or grab hold. But like the skier, we have to make the personal decision to set aside our fears, doubts, pride, and guilt and go with God. He has already sent His Son to save us from our sins—to give us that second chance—but we have to trust in His ability to pull us out of the murky waters of our sin and let Him navigate us through the course of life, to trust in His ability to keep us afloat even when life puts enormous pressure on us.

I grabbed hold of the rope. I allowed the boat to pull me up out of the water. There was no other way for me to win. It was either grab hold or give up. And grab hold I did! Only then could I focus on completing the course set before me and continue on to win the gold.

Likewise, as Christians, we have to allow God to pull us up out of the water and set us on the course He has determined for us.

I know it's not easy. But it's that simple. Getting to heaven isn't about what we can do or how good we are. It's all about Jesus. He has already done everything on the cross. All we have to do is accept what He has done for us and put our trust in Him.

How wonderful to know that we don't have to do anything extra to get to heaven! All we have to do is trust in Him and receive His precious gift of salvation!

What Are We Thinking?

Yet many of us make it so difficult. For one reason or another, we send the boat away. Why?

Is it because we think we're just automatically connected? Perhaps you may believe in God, just as I did, but you don't understand that a relationship with God requires more than just a mere belief in His existence. I can believe the boat is there, but that isn't enough by itself to pull me out of the water and through the course. Even Satan believes in God, the Bible says (James 2:19). We have to act on our faith, grab hold of God, and allow Him to guide us through life.

Is it because we're afraid of giving up our freedom? People feel safe in the water, they know what to expect, and they enjoy thinking they have some control of their destiny. I struggled with this issue for years. I thought if I allowed God to lead my life, who knew where I might end up? Did it mean I'd have to go to the jungles of Africa as a missionary?

Would I have to settle for a boring life with no friends and no fun? My pride caused me to believe that I'd be better off propelling myself through the course the way I wanted to go, that I could handle things just fine on my own. But as you'll read later on, this couldn't have been farther from the truth.

Is it because nothing else has seemed to work, so how could Jesus be any different? So many times I hear people say, "I've tried to ski before, but I couldn't get up." The truth is, many outboard boats and personal watercraft don't have enough power to pull skiers out of the water quickly. So because these people were connected to the wrong power source, their skiing experience turned into a flat-on-their-face disaster. They just got dragged behind the boat and eventually sucked right back into the water. After enough failures they simply gave up, believing that nothing was capable of pulling them out of the water. Similarly, because people often grab hold of substitutes for God's power, they often just drag along in life. And it doesn't take long before they are sucked right back into the rough waters of the world—discouraged and frustrated. They don't realize that true power can only come from God and through His Son, Jesus Christ.

Is it because we don't think we're good enough? One of the most disheartening reasons people don't grab hold of the ski rope is because they don't believe they could ever be a great skier. They've failed at too many things before in life, and they're afraid to risk failing again. Or they may fear that they could never meet the requirements of the course, so they just never try. Some people respond to Jesus in the same way. Perhaps they have emotional, relational, or dependency problems that make it hard to believe God could ever

As Christians, we have to allow God to pull us up out of the water and set us on the course He has determined for us.

Why do we reject God?

Is it because we think we're just automatically connected?

Is it because we're afraid of giving up our freedom?

Is it because nothing else has seemed to work, so how could Jesus be any different?

Is it because we don't think we're good enough?

Or is it because we think we have to understand everything first?

use them. They think they need to straighten out their lives first before they grab hold of Jesus, not realizing that He already loves them as they are, that surrendering to Him is their only path to lasting change. But the guilt, ridicule, and low self-esteem talk even louder. The way to God seems too difficult, too unlikely, too impossible.

Or is it because we think we have to understand everything first? Some people won't put their trust in the boat until they know how it was created, how the rope was made, or how the equipment functions. They want all the information before they decide whether they will connect themselves to the power source. Furthermore, these people want to understand why the driver of the boat would ever allow a skier to go through rough water when he could always find perfect conditions if he wanted to. Haven't you heard people say that about God? They have to know everything about Him—the Bible and creation and prophecy, everything!—before they'll put their trust in Him. They want to understand why God allows people to experience terrible things when—seeing as how He's God—He could always help us avoid them. The Bible is clear, though, that we will never understand how God thinks. His thoughts are not our thoughts, nor are His ways our ways (Isaiah 55:8). Since these people never fully understand God and His ways, they never grab hold of Him. And sadly, they remain in the water forever.

Winners and Losers

Yes, those who grab the rope will have to give up some things. They'll have to take some risks, step outside their comfort zones, and experience some spills.

But you know what? Those who refuse to grab the rope will never know the thrill of waterskiing, of accomplishing feats that used to be impossible for them to achieve, of experiencing the power of the boat pulling them through the water. And likewise, those who refuse to grab hold of Jesus Christ never get to experience the transforming power of God in their lives. They never see God at work, performing miracles all around them. Worst of all, they miss out on an eternity with God in heaven.

If any of the above scenarios describe why you may have previously passed up the rope, I pray that God will use the testimony of my life to help change your mind. I pray that the Scriptures I quote from the Bible will open your heart and mind to the truth of the saving power of Jesus Christ.

And I pray that you will grab hold of Him with all your might.

Please, don't go through life (as I did) bobbing up and down in the middle of life's choppy waters, believing in the power of the boat but never grabbing hold. Don't send God away! Grab hold today and accept His gift of salvation!

If you aren't sure whether you're connected to the ultimate power source, if you aren't sure whether you have made the entrance gates, or whether your heart is "laid up" correctly on the inside, consider what the Bible says:

We are hopelessly lost. From the beginning, man has chosen to disobey God and to follow his own selfish desires. (Remember Adam and Eve?) We have all sinned and fallen short of God's perfect standard (Romans 3:23).

Only God can help us. Because the penalty for sin is death (Romans 6:23), God had to provide a way for our sins to be wiped clean.

He has reached out to us in love. God loved us so much that He sent His only Son, Jesus Christ, as the perfect sacrifice to give us forgiveness of our sin and eternal life (John 3:16).

Jesus is our way—our only way. "God has given us eternal life, and this life is in His Son. The one who has the Son has life. The one who doesn't have the Son of God does not have life" (1 John 5:11–12). Jesus said, "I am the way, the truth, and the life. No one comes to the Father except through Me" (John 14:6).

All we do is believe—and receive. We believe on Him and we come to the realization that we cannot be saved without Him. We acknowledge that we are sinners, ask Him to come into our hearts and cleanse us from our sins. We accept the second chance He gives us for life—abundant life here on earth and eternal life one day in heaven. Believing on Him, accepting His gift, and committing our lives to Him is how we begin to become champions for Him.

Prayer

Thank You, Lord, for giving me a second chance at life. Thank You for being a loving Father who only wants good things for me, a Father who is cheering me through the course of life. Thank You for believing in me even when I often doubt myself. I accept Your gift of salvation by grabbing hold of the rope, Jesus Christ. Thank You for paying the price for my sin through the death of Your Son, Jesus, on the cross of Calvary. I now commit my life to You, and I desire above all else for You to be Lord of my life so that I can ultimately become a champion for You! Amen.

CHAPTER 3

WHO'S YOUR COACH?

I was holding a ski clinic recently in Minneapolis, Minnesota, where I had about thirteen students for the day. My friend, Debbie, who had organized the clinic, was introducing me to all of the participants, when one of them—Lisa—who was sitting at the back of the boat, right behind the engine, leaned forward and said, "I'm sorry, I didn't catch your name." At first we all laughed because we thought she was kidding. But when she kept waiting for my response with her hand held up to her ear, I realized she really *didn't* know my name.

This struck me as a bit strange—not because I expect everybody to know who I am, but here she was at a ski clinic at seven o'clock in the morning, having paid a fair amount of money to be there. What other assumption could I draw but that she really loved to ski . . . and she wanted to learn from me. But at the time, she didn't realize who I was. She was just coming to the clinic on the recommendation of a friend. She trusted Debbie's judgment, and she didn't want to miss out on a fun experience. It wasn't until she got back to shore that she realized what my qualifications were as a ski coach!

Lisa was so embarrassed. But I didn't mind. In fact, I thought it was funny. It reminded me how people are often so eager to do whatever their friends are doing that they really don't think about what they're getting themselves into.

> It reminded me how people are often so eager to do whatever their friends are doing that they really don't think about what they're getting themselves into.

They jump headfirst into things just because someone else is doing it or because they trust the person who told them about it.

How often is this same thing true in the world of religion. People often chase after a particular religion without actually knowing its beliefs and teachings. They listen to their friends and blindly trust their judgments. But unfortunately, many are being led down the wrong path because they're going on nothing more than what people say. Like Lisa, they don't know who they're following . . . just the crowd, whatever feels good and sounds right.

Get This Straight

Because of this tendency of ours, I want to encourage you to take your Bible and search out everything that I proclaim in this book. Don't just take my word for it. Experience it for yourself.

Perhaps you won't believe it's true. That's a personal decision only you can make. But you should still read the Bible for yourself, not just take someone else's word for it.

If you *do* believe the Bible is true, then it only makes sense that you should heed its message, keeping yourself connected to the only power source that can successfully navigate you through life. You should also test what you hear about other world beliefs to see if they square with the Scriptures (1 John 4:1). You need to know what you believe and make sure it's in agreement with the Bible.

I'm telling you, Satan seeks to mislead us and cause us to go astray (1 John 3:7). He has no boundaries to the methods he will use to keep us from having a true relationship with Christ. In fact, he will often worm his way into the church to stir up controversy and division.

We have to be on guard and make sure that our beliefs match up with God's Word. First John 4:5 warns us to beware of religions that are not consistent with the Bible because they are "from the world and therefore speak from the view-point of the world, and the world listens to them" (NIV). People are often told what they want to hear—messages that make them feel good about themselves—but they aren't told what they *need* to hear.

If you *do* believe the Bible is true, then it only makes sense that you should heed its message, keeping yourself connected to the only power source that can successfully navigate you through life.

- *So how can we know that we are not being led astray?*

- *How can we tell if people who claim to be Christians truly are Christians?*

- *How can we know that we ourselves are children of God?*

So how can we know that we are not being led astray?

How can we tell if people who claim to be Christians truly are Christians?

How can we know that we ourselves are children of God?

Distinguishing Marks

The Bible gives us great insight into how we can know if what we hear from another person or religion is truly of God.

Do they declare that Jesus was a real person? First John 4:2–3 says, "This is how you know the Spirit of God: Every spirit who confesses that Jesus Christ has come in the flesh is from God. But every spirit who does not confess Jesus is not from God." If a religion refuses to acknowledge that Jesus was both God and man, that the Son of God actually became a human being and walked on this earth, then according to the Bible, that religion is not in agreement with God.

Do they declare that Jesus is the only means of salvation? The Bible is clear that the only way for a person to obtain access to God the Father is through His Son, Jesus Christ (John 14:6). If Jesus is left out of the equation of salvation, then the equation will never be complete. Without Him—without the perfect, sinless Son of God—there is no sacrificial death. The Bible says, "Without the shedding of blood there is no forgiveness," so Christ was "offered once to bear the sins of many" (Hebrews 9:22, 28). Otherwise, we would have absolutely no way to come into the presence of a holy God. Therefore, it is imperative that Jesus Christ is the foundation of our belief.

And as to whether someone who claims to be a Christian is really

following the Lord, the Bible says that we should be able to recognize the truth of their spiritual state by the fruit they bear in their lives.

This goes for us, too.

"Every good tree produces good fruit, but a bad tree produces bad fruit" (Matthew 7:17). What kind of things are we talking about? Galatians 5:22 says that the fruits of the Spirit are love, peace, joy, patience, kindness, goodness, faithfulness, gentleness, and self-control. These are the things that will begin to surface in a Christian's life and relationships. They'll show up in the way we handle tough situations, in the things we say and do.

Sure, there will be times when we may not be producing as much fruit as we should. But if we truly have Christ in our hearts and lives, the Holy Spirit who resides within us will guide us—over time—to make decisions and choices that glorify Christ (John 16:13–14).

Words to Grow On

It's easier said than done, of course. But the Bible uses the analogy of God being like a vine that contains all the nutrients that the branches need—that's us!—in order to produce beautiful fruit. Just as the skier needs to remain connected to the boat to accomplish feats on the water, Christians have to remain connected to God, or we will wither and fail to produce anything (John 15:5).

And once again, the Bible comes back into play here. One of the best things a Christian can do to remain firmly connected to God is to study His Word. It is imperative that we know how He expects us to live our lives. Why? Because

the only way we can remain in close fellowship with Him is by being obedient to Him. And the only way we can know how to be obedient to Him is by letting Him tell us.

When I coach skiers, I let them know what I expect. When they listen to my instructions and give an honest effort to do what I asked, I know that they respect me and my ability as a coach to lead them through the course. Similarly, God says that we show our love for Him by obeying His commands (John 14:15), by trying our best to be all that He desires.

If someone claims to know God but continually refuses to keep His commands, it's possible that he is not truly a child of God. Ultimately, of course, this is God's business. But the Bible does teach us that a changed heart should result in a changed life. Now, I'm not proposing that Christians are perfect and always obey every command in the Bible. Christians still make mistakes. We are humans with a sinful nature (Romans 7:25b). But sin should not be the norm in our lives, something we continue to do, because this takes us out of fellowship with God.

And let me tell you, being out of fellowship with God is a miserable place to be. The only way a Christian can be content is by living every day for Him.

Just as the skier needs to remain connected to the boat to accomplish feats on the water, Christians have to remain connected to God.